Ode of a Citizen

We are citizens who feel suppressed

We are citizens who feel like nobody is listening

We are citizens of the world who feel like citizens of our space

We are citizens who are muted before we can even formulate a thought

We are citizens drowning in noisy static looking for a life preserver of clarity

We are citizens whose identities are continuously in peril

We are citizens who deserve better

We are citizens, each with our own voice

We are citizens with the power to make things better.

ONE CITIZEN'S WORDS

One Citizen's Words

Christine Whitmarsh

Cover Art:
Julie Jackson

Cover Layout & Design:
Jesse Kebschull

Editing:
Heidi Stroebe and Jesse Kebschull

Christine, Ink. Publishing
www.christine-ink.com

Dedicated to the memory of my grandmother Allene Pitman for the gift of words that has defined my life

One Citizen Thanks...

Heidi Stroebe and Jesse Kebschull for all their talent, dedication and hard work in helping this book finally become a reality

My extremely talented friend Julie Jackson for drawing the beautiful, classy goddess that graces the cover of this book

All my writing clients for allowing me to do for a living what I was born to do anyway

Cristina Perez and Christopher Gonzalez for giving me a chance and for their friendship

Terese and Terry Winson for sharing their business knowledge so generously with me

All my English teachers who made a difference by helping me develop my writing talent early on; especially Mr. Belair, Mr. Berenger and Mrs. Underwood

My friends and family for their support

My sister Karen Whitmarsh for her continuous
encouragement

My late father Alan Whitmarsh, my literary
bloodline and continued source of spiritual
support

My mother Margery Whitmarsh, for her chronic
unblinking support of my creativity, my choices
and a lifetime of chatter

My late grandparents - Allene Pitman for her gift
of words and Douglas Pitman for his gifts of
common sense, values and entrepreneurial
inspiration

God for blessing me with the gift of writing and
Jesus Christ for guiding and feeding that gift

Table of Contents

I. Introduction

II. Words of a Citizen

III. Words of a Nation

I.

INTRODUCTION

About Words…

Words

(1948)

By

Allene Pitman

Words may be inspiring, words may be great.

Words that you use may determine your fate.

Words to some are so confusing

Words may also be amusing.

Words can make you happy and gay.

Words may take your troubles away.

Words can call you a fright,

Or a most beautiful sight.

Words may make you cheerful and very glad.

Instead of tearful and sometimes sad.

Even little words like yes and no.

They can pack quite a blow.

Words can give you a horrid emotion

Or fill you with a tender devotion.

So toss them lightly on your way

And be glad you used them carefully today.

My grandmother, a published poet in New England newspapers during the 1940's and 1950's, wrote this poem in 1948. As a writer today, I am so proud to carry on my grandmother's obvious passion for words. In my favorite of my grandmother's poems *Words* she defined the power and possibilities of words for her era. With this book I hope to do the same for this modern era, when the words we speak and the courage to speak them, is more important than ever.

My entire life and career as a writer has been motivated and colored by my love of words. I often say that our passion and appreciation for the written word will ultimately determine our strength and potential to grow as a society. From the drawings of cave men on walls, the tablets of the Pharaohs and Shakespeare's scrolls, all the way to today's emails and blogs, the possibilities and legacy of a people are largely defined by their most inspirational and lasting bond – their words. As it turns out, and as evidenced by my grandmother's poem honoring her own devotion to words, my passion for words is more than a coincidence. It is a family heirloom.

The infatuation I have with words has always been a tremendous guiding force in my life. Yet it wasn't until my mother introduced me to my grandmother's poetry, nearly a decade after her death that I began to understand where my love of words came from. After all, since a young age I have been voraciously addicted to writing anything that existed to be written about. My grandmother was perhaps my biggest fan. From around eight years old, I found such joy in writing short stories for grandma as gifts, in lieu of slippers or a new bathrobe. Yet, through page after page of my typewritten imagination, my grandmother played no different of a role than any other grandmother. She cherished the gifts, showered me with praise and saved every last word that I wrote. My grandmother never spoke to me about her poems, or even the craft of writing. Instead, she encouraged my gift of words with a smile and a thoughtful, perfectly penned thank-you card.

My mother later shared with me that my grandmother handwrote each story that I gave her a typed version of. We're still not sure if this was because of her passion for the stories, her known passion for handwriting (she won a gold medal for her penmanship as a child) or a combination of both. Today, as the ink on those typed pages begins to fade, I am thankful that because of my grandmother's loving efforts, the stories themselves have not faded. This is the sincere devotion of a grandmother to her granddaughter and a devotion to the words that she cherished.

Thirty years into my life, a life inexplicably (or so it seemed) defined by the power and passion of words, I first read *Words*. By the time I reached the last line, I understood the poem's personal significance in my life. I knew that my grandmother's most special thank-you card for my story gifts was the gift at the root of the stories themselves. Ironically, a gift passed from grandmother to granddaughter that was unspoken, bittersweet - and yet more wonderful than anything she could have ever said to me.

About this citizen...

As a writer and citizen of a more modern era, my version of "Words" is different than my grandmother's. This is my ultimate inventory of musings, philosophy, humor, concerns, poetry, irony and pop culture observations. This is a forum for both basic and complex thoughts, yet always a fun, quick read for opinionated readers or readers seeking to find their own opinions. After all, one of my goals is to inspire the next generation to see life in a different light than the light that constantly glows from their televisions, computer monitors and cell phones that can sometimes be blinding and brain scrambling. This is to be a more honest and thought provoking view of the world. This is to be my personal card catalog of existence.

The string that holds these mini-diatribes together is my overwhelming obsession with words, everything they represent, and their power to mold and shape the way we see and operate in this world. Most importantly, I am focusing on the words that each one of us chooses to represent our own point of view. I am so motivated by the apparent dissipation of literary passion that I've seen through my own little window to the world, particularly by the generations coming along after my own. And as a proud, card carrying member of the famously apathetic "Gen X", that says an awful lot. I can only hope that we are not becoming a society that ends up communicating via instant messaging on cave walls.

I hope that sharing my passion will motivate you to form your own opinions and words, and that you will then be inspired to think about the words that you use to create your identity with every day. Create your own card catalog that represents your life, your beliefs, your thoughts, opinions, poetry – your existence! What do your words mean to you? What do they say about you? Are you really reflecting your view of the world in a way that respects and validates your uniqueness within it? It is your point of view after all, and my greatest wish for you, my fellow citizen of the world, is to become aware of just how special that is.

About being a citizen...

For the most part, we live in a world where we can speak our mind. And in those parts of the world and society where that is not the truth – it is exactly this kind of strength and conviction that will eventually change things. In ancient history, weapons of intellect were far weaker than the sword. Since then, the power of the pen, the voice and the mind have won considerable battles. It is now up to us to win the war.

Why is it, then, that I sometimes get the feeling that the oxygen we breathe is allergic to the words we speak? For me being a citizen means being counted, being acknowledged, being validated – and just plain being in a reality. When we are challenged to balance being a citizen of our own space – mind, body and soul - with being a citizen of the world that surrounds us, it's sometimes hard to find the courage to speak what we're thinking and share it with others.

My aim is to fix that by setting an example in the pages of this book. I don't claim to know the secret to life. Although I have a pretty good idea that it has something to do with being happy – truly happy without any disclaimers. I also don't claim to have the instant solutions to poverty, world peace, lost socks in the dryer, equalizing male and female libidos, ending the urge to destroy ourselves or any other lofty problem reserved for the higher plane intellectuals out there.

Here's what I do have: A very honest, sometimes amusing and frequently controversial perspective on life that I am happy to entertain and provoke you with. In this book, I have managed to wrap my words - thoughts, ideas, humor and more - in brightly colored packages of poetry, jokes, observations, monologues and commentaries. I hope this demonstrates to you the power, creativity, flexibility and possibilities of words. So, have a grand ol' time reading my words, but for Shakespeare's sake use this book as inspiration to surgically extract, acknowledge, validate and communicate your OWN words!

WORDS...

I'm not trying to get you to change your mind - just to speak it!

After all, our brains weren't created on an assembly line, so why should our opinions be?

If my words somehow inspire or provoke you to express your words, then I have done my job as a citizen of this world.

My words are not meant to get you to change your mind or invalidate your words.

My words are meant to inspire you to speak your mind so that others will hear and be inspired to do the same.

Get inspired, get excited or get angry - most importantly, get your words out there for the world to hear!

Say it loud, say it proud

Our words have the power to change the world!

II.

WORDS OF A
CITIZEN

The words in this section introduce

the ideas, personal observations and

issues of a single citizen of our world.

A.D.D…

Attention Deficit Disorder – or Attention Deficit Hyperactivity Disorder - is yet another brilliant choice of words by the notoriously short-sighted American Medical Association. Lengthen the reading time of a 'disorder' already devoted to individuals with the shortest attention span!

To all the parents out there: If your child is tearing up the house, rearranging furniture and turning everything into an art or a craft – it's not called A.D.D. – it's called imagination. And imagination should *never* be medicated.

Adults Only…

Speaking of children - Theme parks are not ACTUALLY for children. If theme parks are for kids why are they screaming like banshees 99% of the time? Why do people take their kids to theme parks when clearly these types of places are for adults only? Think about it: a place full of DMV inspired lines, long hours, inflated prices, public transportation and a definite theme of delayed gratification leading to absolute disappointment once it's over. Joy rides ruled by middle management and staffed by flunkies with pseudo-authority (get on the thing, get off the thing, not until I say) who people actually have to obey!

This place is just as condescending as the companies where these parents work, except they have to pay to go there on their days off. The happy costumes and cake disguise the truth just about as well as "Casual Friday" disguises the reality of work in the corporate world. Clearly these places are not for the impressionable virgin minds of children. Theme parks are simply what happen to life in an office when it's turned inside out by sadists with a very twisted sense of humor.

Education is a wonderful thing – in moderation of course. Just like any other drug, book learning can easily become the equivalent of a chemical crutch. I'm talking about the people who go from bachelor's to master's to PhD to doctorate, frequently forgetting to stop and apply any of their book learning to any viable life skills in between.

In extreme cases, the mind of an educational addict can become so cluttered by abstract theories and random concepts that they can't see the forest for the trees. And worse than that, they have absolutely no idea how to apply that philosophical statement to real life. Even worse, if they get lost in the forest they have to be rescued by an elementary school boy scout.

The education addict risks becoming so distracted by the idea of "knowledge" that they begin relying more and more on other people and outside resources to form the simplest opinions, solve the easiest problems and execute what used to be basic life functions.

They eventually doubt the validity of their own knowledge, intelligence, opinions and ideas (also because of the infamous PC plague) and become walking and talking puppets awaiting instruction from the nearest ventriloquist.

I have a Bachelor of Science Degree from a very good New England University. I am an advocate of higher learning, especially considering the current state of affairs in America. I am also a fan of hamburgers, beer, pizza, nachos, wine and all of life's other wonderful indulgences. My point is a simple one – moderation. When higher education is abused, a mind truly becomes a terrible thing to waste.

Being a Real Baseball Fan...

Regarding the Red Sox-Yankees rivalry from one citizen on the Sox side of the wall:

As much as we generally hate each other, Red Sox and Yankee fans get each other. We despise each other the way that a viciously estranged husband and wife can run into each other in the hallway of family court and laugh at the other couples in the hallway –

yeah, you think you're estranged? We'll show you estranged!

Why baseball anyway? Why this sport? Baseball is more like an outdoor sports bar where the game on the giant plasma screen is extremely lifelike. There's the same drinking, yelling, and partying with your fellow fans while yelling at the players, umpires, coaches and rival fans… only they can hear you. And when someone hits one out of the ballpark you get to scream your head off with 30 or 40 thousand other people. That's what makes the Sox and Yankees a slice above the rest… 40 thousand other people screaming with you. Some other teams' games I've seen are more like a 4th of July picnic that half the town lost their invitations to.

College Preparatory…

Forget college preparatory for just a moment… It's a gimmick. It's a lie to keep high school students in line and give them something to work toward – their "permanent record." This is a nationwide philosophy that current and future victims of middle management

bank on their workers buying into. Simply p~
there were no Emerald City, Dorothy would have
taken over the lease on the dead witch's hut, broken
out the margaritas and had hundreds of instant little
drinking buddies.

College Values...

In the interest of molding young minds with valuable
information, here is my advice to college graduates:

>Everything you learned and were told would define
who you are as a grown-up, especially your major,
makes for nothing more than entertaining
conversation at the company Christmas party.
Seriously, you really thought you were going to use
any of that stuff? You just bought yourself a four
year, $100,000 hangover my friend.

>Unless your career of choice is hooker, you will
never ever have the sex life you had in college for the
rest of your life. It's not physically possible so don't
try or you will injure yourself and possibly others. In
college I was some guy's Wednesday night girl and I

had no problem with that. Now if I'm some guy's yearly girl I'm thrilled.

>Marijuana may help your college homework but unless you have a fruity job (like writer for instance), pot has no real world value to help you up the corporate ladder. If you're a banker or corporate type, smoking pot will probably make your life just seem to suck more. If you're a doctor, especially a surgeon, it will definitely make other people's lives suck more. If you're a lawyer... actually I would encourage lawyers to smoke more weed. It would certainly make life easier for jurors. Imagine: "Uh, this dude's innocent, this dude's soooo totally guilty, I don't remember who the heck this dude is so let's order a pizza and some breadsticks."

>The deep political and philosophical conversations and debates you've been immersing yourself in for the past four years will turn into the following intellectual real world dialogue: "Hi how are you, good and you, another Monday huh, yeah, two days to hump day, you said it, four days til' TGIF, yeah man, any weekend plans, yeah well you know how it

is, catch you later, how about this weather, how 'bout that team, how about that boss, have a good one."

Come to think of it, maybe everyone in the real world is already stoned and I didn't get the memo!

>Multi-tasking is not defined as the ability to hit the snooze alarm while giving your boyfriend a hand job.

Dreadlocks...

Hey Mon! Try removing the dread in your life and making it into dreadlocks. Make the things in life that you fear the most, the things that excite you the most. What's the worst that could happen? Don't answer that.

Fearless...

It takes courage to be fearless because becoming comfortable with yourself is always a tremendous leap of faith.

Genius...

The Genius

He was like Mozart and Picasso. He was no different from all the other great ones who were elevated to such status after their deaths. The young inspired artist who was too intelligent for his own good. The genius, who knew so much about life and what it offered, that it scared, frustrated and angered him.

He was under the mistaken impression that, just because life catered to the average, the ignorant masses, that it could offer him no more than misery and self-hatred.

What he failed to realize, was that in his world of self-hatred and isolation, the bright shining star of potential was fighting to shine through the blackened smog. He did not realize that he was intentionally killing himself from the inside out, while constantly contemplating the best way to kill himself from the outside in.

He was too scared to allow life to be bea
be livable. Contrary to his beliefs, happin...
reject him. He was on a constant path of rejecting
anything remotely good about life. Life wasn't
kicking him in the ass. He was just refusing to be at
peace with it. And that was so much more difficult
than seeing the good and letting it be enough.

Emotional and mental peace with life, unchanged,
gave him naturally what he had been trying to get
from anger, depression and frustration - a reason to
live.

I'm just saying…

Why bother having an opinion at all if you're going to
immediately censor yourself by tacking on the very
popular, maddeningly cowardly disclaimer – "I'm
just saying..." No single phrase in the English
language angers me more! Have some pride in your
words. Don't back peddle in the face of the smallest
amount of resistance. So you have an opinion, so you
say it, so someone else challenges you – who cares?

Stand your ground. Those are your words you just said and nobody has the right to make you take them back. That's exactly what "I'm just saying" is – a take back, a request for a do-over. Can you imagine a kid ever doing that? No way, man! When kids have something to say, they yell it out. Whether it's at the playground, the grocery store, or in the middle of church! So what if everyone stares, gives disapproving looks and clucks? Shucks to them – they're just jealous. If you're going to say something – just say it.

Imperfect Being...

I am schizophrenic.

I am manic-depressive.

I am homicidal.

I am suicidal.

I am a devil.

I am a saint.

I am psychotic.

I am neurotic.

I am stoned.

I am buzzed.

I am drugged.

I am dirty.

I am clean.

I am independent.

I am a child.

I am dreaming.

And I never want to stop.

Lesbianism...

The girl in the white cat suit (or mouse?) looked me up and down skeptically, her painted lips forming a half sneer, half smile. "You're straight?" she laughed. As if the mere concept of heterosexuality in the middle of the West Hollywood Halloween parade was like Liza Minnelli and Barbara Streisand throwing a joint music festival in a red state.

The catty mouse did have a point. I had exchanged my usual prissy image earlier in the evening for this year's costume: the butchiest lesbian of the butch lesbians. I'd like to say it was a dare but truthfully it was merely a suggestion by my lesbian friend and neighbor. Also, in the years since my actual childhood I'd pretty much run out of homemade costumes that non-children can realistically get away with at Halloween. It was either "butch lesbian" or "chick in a white sheet with two holes punched in the top." In PC-crazed So Cal, I thought the sheet idea might be seen more as KKK than BOO. So, butch lesbian it was!

I didn't think much of it, just a typical Halloween, until actually donning the ensemble. First, the ripped camouflage cut-offs... whoa... I suddenly felt like scaling a wall and kicking butt Rambo style! Then there was the man's "wife beater", a knit tank top with no bra. Very interesting - freeing actually! Finally there came the suit jacket and converse sneakers of course - retro-comfy! My neighbor then attacked my recently chopped hair with hair gel and a baseball cap. With my tousled "boy hair", ball cap tilted to the side gangsta style, and a necktie, there I was, suddenly staring at a skinny, rather pathetic looking teenage boy in the mirror. I wasn't wearing a smidge of "Halloween-y" make-up or a crazy get-up, yet to me, the person in the mirror was completely unrecognizable. I couldn't stop staring. I felt so completely like a spectacle on display that I couldn't imagine ever leaving my friend's apartment. And the evening had just started.

In the car en route to West Hollywood, I couldn't stop stealing glances over our driver's (the REAL butch lesbian) shoulder of the boy in the mirror. I suddenly remembered how my mother was convinced I was a boy throughout her pregnancy, calling me "Brett" until the moment of my birth. Mom would be ever so proud tonight.

My second observation was that, after a lifetime of continuous primping, prodding, and perfecting before, en route to, and while going out, this was strange. I was sitting in the backseat with nothing to adjust, no hairstyle to fix, no makeup to touch up, no pantyhose to hitch up, and no skirt to adjust. We were getting closer and closer to our destination – a massive, wild party in the streets of West Hollywood – and I looked the same now as I did when we left the house. Nothing polished about me! I panicked. What would happen when I stepped out of the car into the throngs of costume clad beauty queens?

We arrived and found ¾ of a parking space near the center of the action. One and a half butch lesbians and my friend the lesbian beauty princess stepped out of the car and strutted up the street, a bizarre threesome in the midst of a swarming freak show accessorized by more fried meat vendors than I was able to logically connect with Halloween. For some reason most of the women were dressed as slutty nurses (ironically I had retired as the real thing years before) and men as Michael Myers and drag queens (some of which may not have been costumes).

As we immersed ourselves in the mob, I had a shocking realization. I did not feel "on display" as a fish out of water. In fact, I didn't feel conspicuous at all. Far from it, I actually felt invisible, the proverbial fly on a wall. It may have been because the clothes were so comfortable that I was equally comfortable. And the baseball cap hid most of my face, obscuring my view of the outside world so I was in denial of actually being there. I've never been in a sensory deprivation tank, yet that's what it felt like to me.

Word to my fellow "do-it-up" ladies who would never dream of leaving the house in veritable "jammies" without a bra – it's awesome. Take the experience of hanging around your house in your most comfie clothes on a Sunday afternoon and put it in the middle of a formal party. It may sound akin to the "running down the street naked" nightmare, and it does take a bit of reckless courage, but I highly recommend it if you can ever find such an opportunity without getting arrested or fired.

Another strange observation was that, after far too many years of trying to gain male attention through hair, make-up, clothing, and the other trademarks of a woman, it was completely bizarre knowing that dressed this way there was zero possibility of my getting even a glance from a man. I was more on their side, fashion wise, than I was on my own side. I suddenly found myself thinking about all the times I justified the Barbie getups saying, "I do it all for me!" empowered as can be. If that was the case, than why, dressed like a boy, did I crave male attention more than ever? I looked at my neighbor, dressed to the feminine nines, primed for male attention, with jealousy. Suddenly I realized how great it is to be a woman and how much I missed it.

A few cops on horses, Bush protesters, children in strollers (what?!?), far more sidewalk sausage vendors than I would imagine to be necessary outside of Germany, and a near trampling later, we started running into my neighbor's friends, the real lesbians. According to my friend, what they really meant by their frequently asked question "you're straight?" was, "Please come join us. The grass really is greener on the other side." I have only the most open-minded, compassionate intentions when I say - thanks but no thanks.

After surviving my sexually incognito evening, when the more popular undercover experiment for women seems to be a fat suit, I am very thankful to my friend for the experience. The assumption would be that feigning the opposite sexuality would allow me to explore that sexuality. Instead I gained a deeper understanding of my innate sex appeal as a heterosexual woman. Something was reawakened inside me. Since that night I have felt more comfortable in my skin – no matter how I'm dressed and what's happening with the hair, make-up and pantyhose – than ever before. By extracting my essence as a woman, I was able to study it from the outside in and understand myself on a new level.

By the end of the evening, I learned: lesbian women are empowered to speak their minds without fear of judgment or retribution, they are publicly affectionate without worrying about what anyone thinks and overall, they are concerned about each other's comfort and happiness. It's no accident that "becoming" a lesbian for an evening helped me understand and embrace the very best things about being a straight woman. All from walking a mile in a lesbian's converse shoes!

My perfect man…

He's everything I dreamt of.
My so-called perfect man.

He's funny, smart and handsome.

What's called the perfect man

So why am I so doubting?

When he never holds my hand.

Why am I so lonely?

When we're always making plans.

When we talk it's like he's not there.

When we kiss it's like he doesn't care.

Whether or not he sees me.

Or if he calls again.

Or even he claims to know me.

On that I can't depend.

What could he be thinking?

I'll never understand.

Is it me or is it him?

Why can't I know his plan?

Am I a mistake he made?

Or is he shy and scared?

So my so-called perfect man.

Is still a mystery to me.

It's like I never met him.

To me he's still a dream.

In the meantime how to deal with,

This reality.

Do I leave him, do I keep him?

I wish I knew just what he sees.

If I knew that he cared about me.

I suppose I'd care for him.

But that seems too doubtful.

I can tell it by his stare.

When he looks at me,

His eyes they say we're through.

Why does he seem to care so much?

But never hold me close.

Why do his words they mean so much?

A friendship hug at most.

What I may be seeing.

What I thought could be romance.

May be nothing but good friendship.

With my so-called perfect man.

One Person Play…

Do you ever get the feeling that other people have cast you as an unwilling participant in the one person play of their life? And on top of that, they didn't bother to give you a script. When people create an assumption about you, the next logical step is to create a scene with you in their head. A scene in a play that, well, you've never quite been invited to participate in.

Now that you're aware of that, isn't it much easier not to take what anyone says or does to you personally? You can't control anyone else's theatre so don't try. But what you can do is make sure that you don't unwittingly do the same thing to other people. Your life is your one person play. There is always an audience and a support group of people backstage to help you. But unless someone wants to join you on stage, don't drag them out onto the stage. This also means not to act like a crazy fan and jump onto the stage of someone else's show. Your life is your show. Now, go write, direct and produce it!

Regret...

...is a very covert form of self-destruction. Here's how that chain of logic works.

1. God creates a person with free will
2. You get to choose the person you want to be

3. You make a life choice

4. You later decide that it wasn't a good choice after all

5. Since your time machine is temporarily out of commission you decide that the best course of action is some vague, indefinable thing called "regret"

There is no action item or forward motion associated with this strange state of paralysis. So you hang this state of "regret" onto your self-image and everything that you stand for. Why? Why not just find some value in the choice you made? A lesson, a message… something! Otherwise you're just assigning a random state of self-blame and ultimately self-destruction. And not to just anyone – you're assigning it to YOU, of all people!

Self-Proclaimed Experts…

I love these people who can only do for a living what they are specifically trained or educated in. I call them the - "I have a PhD in exactly what it is that I'm doing now" people. It seems that there were lots and lots of folks throughout history before the concept of ducation came to light, who still managed to survive and even evolve without taking a correspondence course on rubbing two sticks together. You know what I have? A PhD in making-stuff-up-as-I-go-along, from figure-it-out-university.

Situational Identity…

On a day to day basis, are you a product of your situation or of yourself? In other words, are your words and actions truly motivated by what others expect of you or what you expect of yourself? What is it about yourself that you are afraid of exposing to others? Shouldn't being a product of who you are be good enough? If it's not, whose fault is that and what are you going to do about it?

Soooooooooo….

"I went over to his house, soooo…", "The shirt didn't fit, soooo…', "I flunked English class, sooooo."

Sooooo, when did "soooooooooo" become soooo much more than a conversational transition? When did it become an acceptable way to actually end a sentence? Are people soooo completely mentally toxic and bugged out that they literally can no longer complete a real sentence or a complete thought? Soooo....

Reconnecting with your inner words…

Do these exercises first for yourself and then to share with the rest of the world in hopes that others will also reconnect with the words they own that have the power and potential to change the world. I would also encourage you to share your results on the official website for "Words the Movement": www.myspace.com/wordsthemovement

What is your favorite word and why?

What is your most controversial thought or idea?

What is the funniest thing that has ever popped into your head?

III.

WORDS OF A NATION

Welcome to the monologues, diatribes

and quips that influence our lives as

citizens of a nation...

America in particular.

Driving me crazy...

<u>To the tailgater behind me</u>: The good news is - I'll eventually be out of your way. The bad news is - you'll still be a jerk.

<u>To the funeral procession driver in front of me</u>: If I wanted to drive in the Macy's day parade, I'd blow up Charlie Brown and hire a department store greeter to yank his chain.

<u>To the faxing, coffee drinking, smoking, hair curling, boyfriend blowing, pot smoking auto-multi-tasker next to me</u>: Perhaps one of those tasks should actually be... DRIVING?

Fats 4 Fuel....

I have personally figured out the solution to two of our most pressing national problems: obesity and our dependence on foreign oil. Squeamish uber-PC types might want to step out of the room for this bit. Okay, so you may have heard how corn oil makes for an effective fuel alternative. Has anyone yet considered the "lipo" growing safely and naturally in guts, butts and thighs from sea to shining sea, and then suctioned in 90210 and zip codes beyond? And what of the lipo that continues to wiggle and jiggle its way down Main Street, USA? I say, just because the suctioning part hasn't occurred to those ready sources of fatty fuel, that shouldn't stop us from doing some automotive lipo mining. It is our duty, after all, as Patriotic Americans, to reduce America's dependence on foreign oil – by increasing our dependence on fatty oils here in our homeland. If they can do it with corn oil, they should be able to do it just as easily with French fry, fried chicken, cheeseburger and chocolate cake oil... Fats for freedom!

Ga, ga, goo, goo...

To all the parents who feel the need to speak to their children as if they are globs of un-evolved amoeba with no grasp of what actual words and formulated thoughts are: You know the 40-year-old virgin that still lives with his parents and loves to suck on either a nipple or a joint? That's your future kid.

Holiday Card Exchange...

As I purchase, pen and postmark my "holiday" greeting cards, praying desperately that I have guessed the recipient beliefs, religions and general holiday opinions correctly, I can't help but wonder if there's an easier way. It suddenly just occurred to me – we may have the whole holiday card exchange procedure completely backwards.

The custom is to send cards to people based on what you know (or guess) their beliefs are and in some cases selecting the politically correct generic "happy holidays" as a reasonable safety net. This custom, I believe, may have led us down the "slippery slope" towards the widespread elimination of Christmas, Kwanzaa and anything else that might be deemed offensive, should a seasonally specific card end up in the wrong hands.

Here is what I propose for a hassle free holiday season and a harmonious new society of integrated, accepted and respected beliefs. I propose a radical new system of holiday card exchange for a radical shift in the way we treat each other. From now on, we should send holiday cards that share *our own* seasonal beliefs, whatever they may be (create your own cards as necessary), with the card recipient. For instance, as a Christian I would share that important part of who I am to friends, family and loved ones by sending cards that say (brace yourselves PC types) – Merry Christmas!!! This is certainly *not* to disrespect other people's beliefs as is the common societal notion. Instead this is my way of sharing information with others in hopes that they will do the same, thus sharing a cherished piece of their own lives with me.

I personally would love to share in the beliefs and values of my friends, colleagues, customers, family and loved ones. I think this would be such a wonderful annual gift. Also, I would love nothing more than to decorate my mantle with a colorful, dynamic collection of greeting cards and belief systems. I would love to have Christmas cards side by side with Hanukkah, Kwanzaa and Ramadan cards. What a brilliant way of acknowledging and respecting other people's beliefs and helping to share in them! Think about how my new card exchange system would help to reduce prejudice and religious intolerance. What do you say? Let's buck the system and share our beliefs openly with others in favor of peace and harmony on earth!

Home Depot Olympians…

Is anyone else horribly depressed by the Home Depot commercials that always air during the Olympics, *bragging* about how many Olympians work for them? Seriously, one week these people are on TV in an international parade as American athletic heroes, and the next week they're in an orange smock, helping some crusty old guy find a widget? Isn't there something else that United States Olympians are qualified to do other than hurtling down an icy hill or making keys? I have to say – for Olympians, these people do not impress me as ambitious. I think that in their off time they should be automobile test dummies, roller coaster testers, replacements for the original NASA monkey - or speedboat captains. Let's get our Olympians out of the smocks and onto the docks!

Hollywood Wanna-Do…

That's right – not "wannabe", but "wanna-do", short for "what I really wanna do."

The "what I really wanna" is a generally nocturnal creature. Well, that's when they're in their element. Apparently between hanging out at Starbucks and attending the occasional classes by self-proclaimed experts and anointed idols of the "what I really wannas", the creature is allegedly doing what "they really wanna" do. It's easy for the untrained observer to get the impression that what "they really wanna do" is actually better defined more as what they really don't wanna do. In other words, the hours of their day that count are any hours not spent working their day job.

They are a tricky breed of stealthy creatures. You might be innocently going to get your morning coffee at Starbucks on your way to a job that you are more or less content with – heck you might even actually like your job – and bam! The wild unpredictable "what I really wanna" springs out from behind the counter and rather than take your order – bam! – your friendly "what I really wanna" stealthily spots the screenplay under your arm – uh, oh – "Non-fat vanilla grande latte please" – sure, sure – so hey, you know what? – groan – I REALLY wanna – no, please just make my latte – do, is be an actress! Ahhh! That's lovely. I'm all for it, really I am. But until then, can you find the appropriate emotional preparation to be in the moment with me now?

It's fairly apparent that virtually no citizen of Hollywood, CA and surrounding entertainment-oriented townships is actually doing "what they really wanna do." Well, at least for most of their working hours anyway. A self-respecting waitress in Rhode Island will introduce herself, "Hi, I'm Karen and I'll be your server today." In Hollywood, you're bound to get, "Hi, I'm Karen and I'll be your server but what I really wanna do is act… Just so you know." Thanks for the heads-up Karen, now I know that my service will suck today right off the bat. Thanks for taking out the guesswork Karen. One of these days I'd like to respond, "That's great Karen but while you're acting as my server can you please dig up the motivation to get my order right and do the appropriate emotional preparation to avoid dumping food on me?"

A vital lesson for any "what I really wanna do": Nobody cares about what you wanna do except you. Don't rack up years of the "what I really wannas." Learn how to find even a tiny bit of pleasure, knowledge and personal growth in what you are now. Stop screaming at me about the time "wasted" in your waitress apron versus the onstage apron of a theater stage. I've been in both places. What it comes down to is that work is a privilege. Earning money for contributing a piece of your self is truly a bit of luck that the residents of many countries would saw off a limb to obtain.

This does not mean that I want you to take one iota of passion away from your precious and valuable "really wanna." Very few things in life excite me more than people who are passionate about their dreams and pursue them lock, stock and barrel. But in the event that the gods of the "really wanna" do not immediately start spewing out million dollar doubloons at you like a Y2K ATM gone mad, don't let that be a reason to write off your "day job life" and become the walking, breathing dead. There are gems to be uncovered in everything you do. The sooner you unearth them, the sooner you will really do what you really wanna do!

If only we'd thought of this…

A Native American on a horse sits near the U.S.-Mexico border in the near future, watching as the new great wall is being built. Over his head, is a classic cartoon thought bubble where he has his own vision with the caption "If only we'd thought of this!"

In his vision it is the year 1620 on the coastline of Massachusetts. In the distance the Mayflower is approaching. In front of us, however, the locals are hard at work building a wall along the coastline. One

Native American sees the boats, stops and says to another: "Damn immigrants."

New Torture Methods...

I read somewhere that the United States government is constantly looking for new and humane ways to interrogate prisoners of war. When was the last time that the government sent officials to visit an immensely popular American theme park around closing time? Hordes of wailing, beyond exhausted, completely pissed off children being bodily dragged towards the parking lot by their near suicidal parents. Gee, you think perhaps round-the-clock tape recordings of this high pitched symphony of horror might elicit some prisoner confessions? Better yet, let's hook up the tape to the world's biggest amplifiers and blast it into every cave in Afghanistan. If the enchanting sounds of Capitalists at play can't smoke out Bin Laden, I'm not sure what can!

Nipple Aversion…

Forget about the obvious censorship issues and insanity exposed by one partially exposed nipple. Whether at a Super Bowl show or during feeding time on a local park bench, I prefer to look at the great American nipple controversy from a different angle.

It should be noted that network television has no problem airing images of charred corpses of American contractors dangling from a bridge in Iraq, reality show contestants vomiting after attempting to ingest animal digestive tracts, and baseball players hawking huge loogies of bodily fluids across the field. But a natural human body part? God forbid. What message must this send to the next generation of body conscious young women? Kill it, spit it up, spew it out – but don't you dare take it off young lady because that is what's really disgusting. The body God gave you – that's what's *really* wrong so cover it up and while you're at it, be ashamed, be very very ashamed at this horrible vehicle that is carrying you around. Because we know that you don't spend enough time obsessing over it anyway. Let's give you more reasons to be embarrassed by your body.

Conservative types frequently express their fears that society is constantly skiing out of control down a slippery slope to into hell (or "California" as they call it). Here's one for even the slipperiest of slippery slope fanatics: embarrassed about nipples today, embarrassed about everything else tomorrow, with a raging case of anorexia or bulimia a strong possibility for the day after that.

Sure, that's an outrageous assumption... A slippery slope can go both ways my friends. I just wish more people would take advantage of this fact, stop and hurl some snowballs of logic at the bullies at the top constantly warning everyone else about avalanches.

Plastic Money...

As much as I enjoy playing *Monopoly*, I am well aware that the money is not real. During my brief stint as an owner of plastic money called credit cards, the circumstances felt strangely similar. It was then that I realized buying things with money I hadn't yet earned would never feel quite right to me. And then it occurred to me: I take such pride in working for every single penny that I spend. Using plastic money – an advance where an option exists to "get out of it", the other option being a lifetime of misery from guilt and collector phone calls, would never be acceptable for me.

What happened to the connection between working and therefore earning the living for the life you live? Credit cards are a way of denying the reality that hard work is connected with money. We as a nation and as individuals need to stop living on borrowed money and instead focus on earning money the old fashioned way – rolling up our sleeves and getting to work.

Reality shows and lotteries are simply adding to the smokescreen of delusion that money can be free. In those cases, it can. But eventually the game ends, you realize that the hotel on Boardwalk is a small plastic pawn, the fake money goes back into the box, and it's time to face reality again, instead of faking it.

Putting words in my mouth...

How dare you tell me what my words mean?

How dare you say that because I am against a sovereign slaughter that I am less than the patriotic American I have been for every moment of my life?

How dare you, as I weep tears of pride at the beauty and meaning of my national anthem and tears of heartbreak at the barbaric actions of my nation?

How dare you pray to the same Jesus Christ as I do – a being of love, forgiveness and teaching – when your actions go completely against that beauty?

How dare you judge me lest you be judged – and then when are you are judged do nothing but deny your crimes?

How dare you act out of power hungry greed in the name of the love for America and God and humanity?

How dare you attempt to redefine my values for your own self-interest?

How dare you!

Psycho Political...

Notice to the conservative media and the GOP (or as medical science refers to them: conjoined twins separated at birth): people who have an opinion that happens to be different than yours are not crazy, conspiracy theorists, mentally unhinged, psychiatrically unbalanced or walking and talking incarnations of evil. They are people with different opinions than yours. This does not mean the world is coming to an end. This does not mean that they are all liberal boogey men whose sole purpose in life is to terrorize you. Being a thinking person with the ability to come to an alternate conclusion than the one being spoon fed from the television set, does not place someone "on the enemy's side." It simply means that you are not omnipotent and not everyone has to agree with you. It means that you are a regular human being and what you're saying is simply your opinion – just like this entire book is simply a collection of my opinions. Yet for some reason, when you state your opinion and somebody disagrees, you suddenly turn into a stoner who thinks his cat is out to get him.

Double your dosage or you'll end up sounding like the entire cast of Scooby Doo. Watch out Shaggy, the big scary ghoul is gaining on us! The big scary ghoul, of course being a kindly old shopkeeper who is simply fed up with a bunch of stoners running around creating a false sense of drama because they have no life otherwise.

Your cable news network is already so terrified of its own tail that the sun coming up in the morning requires a highly dramatic flashing alert. Perhaps this network's vending machines should start carrying individual packets of tranquilizers before their on-air personalities become completely unbalanced, spin their way out of control and take half their viewers with them into a vortex of insanity.

Ultimate Self-Help…

Here we are, lying spread eagle in the wasteland of the self-help movement. Some were helped, albeit briefly. Others saw the light and allowed the gospel of self-help to transform their lives, and unfortunately the lives of everyone around them. And still others simply wound up transforming their bookshelves into a hyper-ecstatic collection of – "Yes you can do it, I swear to God you can do it, believe it, do it, who needs sleep, yes, yes, yes!!"

Meanwhile, there is a segment of the population that has recently made their voices heard. These people rejected the self-help movement while it was happening because it wasn't helping them then and now they just downright loathe it because it's *still* not helping. They have quickly gone from a state of neutral, passive self-loathing ("life sucks, then you die") to the realization that nobody was listening to them and nobody cared that they personally thought that their life sucked. We now have a group of extremely pissed off Americans on our hands. They may have been neutral before, now they are passionate, fist pumping, self-hating angry about their lives and they are hell bent determined to let the world know about it.

The television army of rah-rah gurus is doing their best to quell this tide, telling them to be responsible for their anger – own it so it won't own you. I have a feeling that's just pissing them off even more. Watch these people when they are guests on talk shows, dragged kicking and screaming to the studio by a spouse who has threatened to withhold sex (or withhold abstinence in some cases). They just look pissed. Pissed at the host, their spouse, the studio audience and the poor production assistant tasked with bringing them water on the commercial breaks.

Here is what the NEW self-help movement should be. I think it's the only thing that will save us all…

ULTIMATE SELF-HELP!
Sunday! Sunday! Sunday!
Bob has a sucky job as an office temp and a wife who won't do him!

Fred has a lifelong grudge against all the car mechanics, grocery checkers and technical support people who are clearly out to get him and make his life miserable!

Their wives have tried the motivational tapes, the self-help-a-thons and a bald Texan telling them to 'get real'!

Well Bob and Fred have found a whole new way to get real and help themselves once and for all...

This Sunday, Bob and Fred will go head to head in a completely fenced in cage – and beat the holy crap out of each other!

That's right, forty years of anger will all come out, this Sunday, Sunday, Sunday and once and for all, put the final nail into the coffin of the self-help movement!

You're fired, Mr. Bush...

The problem with George W. Bush is that no one ever bothered to give him a job description before he started his job as president. When people are hired they are supposed to get a job description and a proper orientation. Mr. Bush received neither.

Instead, his macho chauvinist pig bosses thought it better to stick him in the lobby like any other trophy secretary, with one purpose and one purpose alone: Sit down, shut up, cross your legs and smile pretty. Most importantly though, whenever anyone asks you a serious question simply giggle, excuse yourself – and go get the real boss!

Reconnecting with your inner words...

Why are *your* words valuable in today's world?

How would you describe the language of America to an alien visitor?

IV.

WORDS OF A SOCIETY

And finally, the piece de resistance.

The words, thoughts and provocative

ideas that will hopefully shape our

future as a society, now and in the

future.

Caffeinated Cinema...

I'm Christine and I'm a coffee addict. I don't just mean drinking it or the buzz of it. I'm talking about the brewing ritual, packaging, aroma, coffee houses and the word coffee itself. I celebrate the entire culture of coffee beans being plucked, ground and mixed with steaming water, poured into a personally eclectic mug and the cosmic swirl of creamer. I can't even watch the depiction of coffee on television or in film without experiencing an involuntary spasm of intense longing and pleasure.

Perhaps that's because in television and film coffee represents so much more than a beverage. It's not the caffeine intake either. Soda, pills, chocolate and many other methods of injecting the buzz work just the same. However, when coffee is used in a cinematic scene it is generally for a provocative reason somehow related to the storyline, meant to heighten, reveal or conceal.

In cinema, coffee often acts as the barometer of the scene, reflecting through the nature of its portrayal the way in which the cinematic moment is to be interpreted by the audience. The support group scene from "Fight Club" comes to mind, in which Helena Bonham-Carter's character impassively overflows her Styrofoam cup of coffee under the bleak lighting of hopelessness where the donuts aren't the only thing stale in the church basement. This simple gesture places a wordless exclamation point on what we already know of her character. This is a woman who experiences life at dangerous extremes and doesn't give the slightest damn as to what the norm is and who made it that way.

In light of coffee's ritualistic addictive quality, it's no surprise that in "Requiem for a Dream" coffee is included in a montage including cocaine, heroin and speed. What would the Jamestown settlers think? Come to think of it, they might be too stoned from Early America's other little cash crop to notice.

Coffee in the cinematic diner scene (and I'm reaching beyond "Alice" here) generally represents scenes pivotal to relationship subplots. It reveals scenes in which critical information is revealed, sometimes outright and sometimes covertly. Gaps are bridged in characters' lives and issues suddenly become clear with the induction of caffeine. In the "Mulholland Drive" diner scenes, cheap black coffee is sipped anxiously from dirty white mugs as perspectives are tampered with, leaving the audience to wonder what, beyond the authenticity of the house beverage, is real.

Another cinematic example of distorted perception is the film "Memento", where the story goes backward and an amnesiac adamantly moves forward. Critical information is exchanged over diner coffee – several different times. We find ourselves in the same diner over that same cup of black coffee, over and over, learning something slightly different each time about the characters and truth of what is really going on.

In "Pulp Fiction", coffee literally fuels the pulp of the fiction as plans are both hatched and foiled over diner coffee. Like everything else in the film, coffee is taken as seriously as a heart attack, and even leads to a brief post-murderous argument between Tarantino, playing the gangster enabler from the valley, and our anti-heroes, in regard to acceptable java quality.

In a more family friendly diner with far less biblical gunfire, Marty McFly from "Back to the Future" finds that some things never change. Much to his relief, he finds black coffee to be the last familiar bridge that has transcended the 30 year gap between his parents' lives and his own. The Twin Pines mall may still be a tree farm out of "Deliverance", Coke in a bottle, the less favorable form of caffeine, might be the only thing that doesn't twist, and Billy Zane might still be a one-line-per-movie actor, but at least coffee is still around to keep Marty in his perpetual state of "heavy" bug-out.

In Beantown's favorite buddy film, "Good Will Hunting", one friend (Ben Affleck) drives up in front of another buddy's (Matt Damon) gated shack every morning with a ride to work and a Styrofoam of Drive Thru coffee in tow. Might this represent Affleck's caffeinated motivation to drive young Will out of his comfort zone, to the bigger and better things that he knows his buddy to be capable of? Later in the film,

Affleck and the other Southie buddies even go to the extent of buying Will a car so he can go through his own damn drive thru for the Styrofoam coffee. Instead, Will discovers a more addictive oral stimulant – an English pre-med student with a Florence Nightingale syndrome. "Gotta see about a double grande non-fat latte" might not have won the Oscar. Some things, even a good cup of coffee can't compete with.

Back in the comfort of my living room, I suck out the last drop of caffeinated nectar, watching from a safe distance as the movie couple in the diner tearfully breaks up. Good God, their coffee is definitely ice by now; it's painful for me to watch such abuse. And what happened to the waitress with the steaming pot? Ever notice how the overeager waitress from the beginning of the scene has apparently gone on severance by the final act of the breakup? Extreme close up of a wedding band being dropped into the stained white mug… Fade to black.

Campaign Stickers on Mini-Vans...

If the campaign sticker on your mini-van is older than
the mini-van itself –
The election is over and so is your sex life.

Celebrated Citizens...

A hypothetical memo to America from its celebrities
Art is, and has always been, merely a reflection of
society. If you don't like what you see – change it –
but don't blame the people holding up the mirror.
We're just a bunch of wackos who make up stories,
find some grown up kids to act them out and then
film them for a living. We're a bunch of freaks that
have decided not to grow up, make careers of it, and
then proceed to make the other 98% of the population
who has grown up, jealous of us. They watch us on
TV, in movies and at award shows living in our little
fantasy world, not looking like them at all, living
completely different lives than them and they treat us
like precious little puppets in a snow globe.

By choosing to be artists, we obviously have given every single person in the world a personal invitation into our homes, our lives and our souls. If we have to endure being followed, harassed, gossiped about and insulted, it's our own fault because by wanting to create art, we obviously wanted to be stalked by strangers.

Since we seem like fantasy people living in a fantasy world, they feel it is okay to treat us like their scapegoats. If they feel overweight, ugly or boring, it's out fault since we don't seem that way at all. If their kids are acting out and misbehaving, it's our fault for setting bad examples for THEIR kids to follow. If the crime rate goes up and more people start shooting one another, it's our fault for giving them the idea. Hollywood makes up about 2% of the population, yet the other 98% can't seem to make a decision without us. We must be the most powerful minority that has ever existed.

Watch who you make into your idols America; we are your children who never grew up. Don't look to us for guidance on how to look, how to act and how to raise your children. Find a better group to look up to. Perhaps a group that makes up more than 2% of your population.

God is not……

God is not your personal butler.

God is not your career strategist.

God is not your maid.

God is not your parking attendant.

God is not your cranky old neighbor whom you have a lifelong grudge against.

God is not your travel agent.

God is not a lottery commissioner.

God is not your therapist

God is not your pharmacist.

And finally…

God is not a genie in a lamp - so don't rub him the wrong way.

Good vs. Evil...

"Is man inherently good or evil?"

This eternal question was pondered in *Lord of the Flies* and has been hashed over in most philosophy classes since. Here's a better idea. Instead of *selecting* the answer, why don't we elevate our level of enlightenment and *create* the answer? After all, majority rules, right? As a species – let's choose the higher road. Sure it takes strength to stay out of the usual muck and mire of jealousy, gossip, revenge and every other negative behavior. It is significantly easier to give in to temptation than it is to rise above it and say – "I don't want to do this because as human beings we don't need this kind of behavior representing and ultimately categorizing our species." Let's take the inherent good vs. evil choice into our own free willed little hands. I choose the high road. I choose to rise above the people who wish to bring me down into their murk, their mire, their drama and whatever contract they've made with themselves that makes that kind of negativity acceptable. That's what I choose. What do you choose?

IM'ing our way back to illiteracy…

I find it ironic that back in the laborious days of quills and inkwells, where the craft of writing must have been an exercise in "dip and write" patience, the writings were literate, prolific and wonderfully worded. Today, in contrast, light little keypads of all shapes and sizes make communication a breeze, yet are most commonly used to tap out choppy little Morse code messages like – LOL, BRB and L8R. Abbreviations and acronyms are somehow replacing words. Except that if you don't know which words the abbreviations are abbreviating – it's not an abbreviation.

Remember, nobody is immune to illiteracy. It doesn't matter whether you're in the Deep South with an outhouse for a toilet or in the finest Beverly Hills mansion with the finest Palm Pilot on the market. If you don't understand why language exists and the importance of words in defining who we are as human beings, illiteracy is a plague that threatens to wipe out future generations of thought before they are even born.

Independence...

Independence is one of the most highly rated and most threatening characteristics that a person can possess. After all, the personal traits, virtues and characteristics that people wish for the most are ones that they will attack the most viciously in others. These attacks are sometimes conscious, often unconscious, passive or aggressive, but as far as our mind is concerned, it's quite deliberate and quite carnal. If I can't have what I want but will never consciously develop it in myself (because I'd therefore have to take responsibility for being it), then damn you for flaunting it. Of course that's not the case, but if the perception is clouded by fear and self-doubt, the viewpoint tends to be a bit askew.

Independence is having unclouded 20/20 vision when it comes to who you are. Who everyone else is – isn't your concern.

Manufactured Imagination

The other day I pulled up to a mega-electronics store only to find a mega-line of the fanciest tents and campsites that money can buy, winding around the store. Had I accidentally arrived at L.L. Bean or the line for tickets to a rock concert? It couldn't be the latter, as my understanding of ticket waiting line accommodations was more Woodstock then a Beverly Hills 90210 camping trip. No, these deluxe, expensive pop tents belonged to the population of kids eagerly awaiting the release of the latest deluxe, expensive electronic video game. The latest incarnation of pre-packaged imagination, pre-created and pre-imagined for your child's playing convenience. This seems sad, allowing all the gaming creators to have all the fun, making up the stories, developing the characters, selecting the colors, backgrounds and music. What's left for the kid? Basically, a really fast paced, flashing personal slightly interactive movie. What's the fun in that?

It's not that I object to the invention itself, the technological progress or the overall intention behind computerized creativity, or as I call it, manufactured imagination. It's just that when a highly evolved vehicle for the entertainment of children provides the end result of the imaginary experience vs. providing the *elements* of imagination, the old-fashioned way, I have some concerns. You remember the elements of imagination, right? During my childhood they included complex inventions such as pots, pans, wooden spoons, empty appliance boxes turned cardboard condos, crayons, a box of chalk with a clean driveway, pencils and an ample supply of blank paper. I had some real toys too. However, because of my mother's choices to supplement the manufactured imagination with the elements of imagination, I credit her with the creative spirit of imagination that fuels everything in my life today. Yes, I work in a creative industry where that spirit is required to make a living. So, is it just a lucky coincidence that my mom instilled this spirit in me? Or is it the reason that I work in this industry? You decide, but I've already come to my conclusion – and it wasn't a hard one.

When a child is given the ingredients of an imaginary experience, they are placed at the beginning of a wondrous new journey. This is an adventure that engages their mind, body, soul and senses in a bold attempt to quite literally make something out of nothing. Imagination strengthens problem solving skills, inspires creativity in choices, broadens life perspective and heightens the experience of life. All this results just by starting with the basic elements of an imaginary experience and letting the child take it from there.

So you can imagine how, when that experience is handed to the child on a shiny, computerized silver platter, most of the imaginary experience is cut short before it ever begins to take shape. The flashing adventures have been pre-determined, the empty lines filled in with beautiful colors (talk about ruining your kid's coloring book by coloring it first), the music selected and every other ingredient of the most fantastic imaginary journey have already been created. What is left for the child to create? Or in adult terms similar to the ones they will face later in life, what is the problem that remains to be solved?

Parents who replace raw creativity, a blank slate, with a completed product, are robbing their children of one of the most important pieces of childhood – the imaginary experience. They essentially are putting their kids at the end of a dead end street

If you are still underestimating the importance of a strong, well-formed imagination consider this: One of the key findings of the federal commission that investigated the tragedy of 9-11-01 was, **"This was a failure of policy, management, capability and, above all, a failure of imagination."**

Medicating Human Nature...

With nimble, strong and flexible limbs, a strong back, supple muscles and a multi-faceted brain, I think it is quite clear that the human body is very conducive to physical activity – work. I realize this may be a radical notion to an emerging society that is nearly allergic to the mere thought of work. Why work when you can pin your financial future on the paper lottery, the reality television lottery, the plastic money lottery, the entertainment industry lottery or any other fictitious means to an ultimately fictitious end? And yet we have talked ourselves into believing that we have made our peace with this new reality. A reality where physical labor has been replaced by automated servitude. We don't engage in a great deal of physical labor (as much as we are designed for anyway) in our daily lives, so is it any wonder that pills have replaced natural sleep patterns, suppressed natural libidal urges and temporarily allowed our digestive systems to function normally? Why do we suddenly need chemicals to live normal healthy lives? Has that occurred to anyone else? Has it occurred to anyone that this might not be particularly normal to rely on a different medication for each of our normal activities of daily living? I'm not suggesting that we all revert to constant physical labor for the sake of physical labor. Just consider this: If beings so obviously designed for work eliminate that concept completely from their lives, as their bodies and minds scream resistance, who will ultimately win this battle?

Multiple Births...

A message to the prolifically reproductive
Quantity doesn't equal quality. Seven morons do not equal one Einstein. Quit while you're ahead. For instance, when you're playing the video slots and you get four aces, you cash in, get your butt off the stool and go back to your room and order room service. You don't keep playing because you know the next hand will be a two and an eight off suit – completely useless. And yet when people have one kid who has all the necessary extremities, body parts, no apparent defects and isn't terribly ugly, they feel obligated to let it ride! Trust me people – the next kid ain't gonna be no **nū'klē-ər** scientist and the one after that... well, does the name George W. Bush ring any bells of horror? Believe me, sex can be just as fun when future Britney Spears aren't being cooked up!

The Perfect Rose

So beautiful and perfect like a delicate rose.
A rose that is rotting on the inside

A rose whose roots are withering away, far below the ground where nobody can see

Nobody except those who look closely

Those who notice, as the smallest leaf dies and floats quietly to the ground so not to attract attention

The perfect, lovely rose.

Admired by the grass and dandelions that surround her

The grass longs for her splendid color and breathtaking scent.

The dandelions yearn for her soft silken petals and tall sturdy stalk.

Meanwhile, the rose continues to grow bravely upward, praying for the sun to give her the strength that she so desperately needs.

Praying for the ground to hold her stalk straight
and strong

But they were all too busy admiring her to help her.

Those who were close to her, spent their time wanting
to be like her instead of wanting to save her.

So when she suddenly wilted and fell to the ground in
one agonizing moment

When her beautiful red petals suddenly turned brown
and broke from her fallen withered stem.

Those who could have saved her stood by in disbelief
and mourning.

 Not understanding what had happened to their lovely
ornament.

Forever mourning the death of their beautiful, perfect,
delicate rose

Sacrificing for the Future

This is not a favorite topic of my generation and adjacent generations. Not to get all Tom Brokaw on you, but there appears to be quite a gaping rift between generations past and generations present and future. Past generations in America have sacrificed for future generations. Was their motivation one of virtue, patriotism and selflessness? Or was it simple necessity for the sake of personal and community survival? Perhaps they didn't know of another option or if they did, it didn't occur to them to exercise it. Or perhaps the things asked of them by their community, government, society and world blended seamlessly with the more nurturing, familial values of the time.

Maybe people in past generations, during historic trials and tribulations, didn't think of things like rations, mandatory blackouts, the draft and supporting community values like mom and pop stores (even if it meant higher prices) as "sacrifices." Maybe these were things they did to ensure that there would be a nation and a world for future generations, generations they were voluntarily bringing into the world.

And now we, the present generations, continue bringing new generations into this world. So many so that even as I write this I can barely wrap my mind around the number of new citizens who will need an environment to survive in, a country to speak freely in and a planet to evolve in. What are we sacrificing so that future generations of citizens may survive and thrive? In order to live in a world even remotely similar to this world, future generations will need: an ecosystem, an economic infrastructure and an effective sense of security.

Now picture the well meaning mother of many, frantically preparing her brood for a Saturday shopping trip. In the background, her husband idly flips through the news stations on TV: an environmental documentary warning of the dangers of our mere existence, a White House press conference announcing the latest constitutional edits, an announcement that the official national mega-mart has now expanded from offering health insurance and voter registration and is now an official federal host of the guest worker program complete with a social security card printing operation in the employee lounge and citizenship tests in the sporting good section next to the ammo case. All of the stories seem important and interesting, yet also very far away from the reality of life under this family's roof. So, the mom and her brood head out to the local branch of the mega-mart in her giant SUV so she can stock up on mega-cheap goods made in countries that are now mega-rich from the mega-outsourcing we've handed them on a mega-platter. She rolls her gas guzzler into the parking lot, pretending not to see the picket line protesters.

They are objecting to the recent attempts by the mega-mart to underbid the once familial mom and pops in order to gain control of the global marketplace. The problem with that theory is that once everyone else is out of business, the last retail powerhouse left standing will have Carte Blanche to do whatever they want, treat their employees however they want and charge their customers whatever they want.

But to the SUV mom today, the protesters are mere distractions and the store is a convenient one stop warehouse of value with no immediate repercussions on her family's micro-existence. Today, the mom is simply taking care of the needs of her family, which of course is an admirable and indeed familial virtue in itself. The needs of her present are more important than the needs of her children's and grandchildren's future.

Today that mega-mart is a source of mediocre quality, low cost goods. Tomorrow it has become the sole source of goods and services to feed a greedy nation. Without the competition it has methodically eliminated, since its conception under the guise of "value" and "family values", the path has been cleared for this superpower to rise and conquer what is left of the economic landscape of our country.

Today, that SUV is a safe and convenient method of shuttling her children and possessions from point A to point B. Tomorrow, the SUV has become an oil embezzling weapon of massive destruction for terrorist nations who truly know how to hit us where it hurts. As if that's not enough, the SUV and others like it are the reasons why meteorologists will eventually become unable to predict anything about the rapidly changing weather and like the rest of us will sit back and watch, waiting for the other shoe to drop. The course of action for any impending natural disaster will be impossible to chart because the massive scale of impending destruction will be far too great to manage.

Scientists and the government have finally agreed upon one simple principle – we've waited too long and now that ship has sailed. In this situation, what else is there really left to say about the far too innocuous phrase "climate change"? Something this potentially dreadful seems too important to get lost in a petty squabble of politics and personal liberties to drive whatever you want, use resources however you want and take advantage of the planet however you want. Has anyone stepped back and looked at the big picture and seen what our petty squabbles have cost us? Because the planet doesn't care about us; The planet would let out one giant sneeze and shake us off itself like the boogers we are if it had the chance. The planet is simply allowing us to sit on it as long as want. But when we take it upon ourselves to crap on that privilege, do you honestly think the planet will lose any sleep over it?

Of course that mom and others like her have the right to own that SUV and run their households however they please here in the free world. But if we really believe that the consequences of our damage is just a hot button political issue under debate that really isn't as serious as it's cracked up to be... then we are just fooling our children and grandchildren. And somehow I don't think they'll get the joke.

Today, the toxic waste produced daily by our environmental, ethical, social, economic, security and civil rights decisions, may seem harmless and inconsequential, its true ramifications in the far off future. But when that future comes and those future generations come of age and the inevitable question that has been asked throughout the ages is asked once again – "What did our ancestors sacrifice to create this life that we have today?" – What will the answer be?

Sanity vs. Insanity...

Imagine a world where the characteristics of sanity versus insanity are defined. That's right, just defined for the sake of being defined. What is normal and abnormal is simply determined. How can we be so sure? Should historical precedent be the decider? The very clinical determination as to whether or not one may cause harm to himself or others seems to have run out of gas and objectivity since it was first established hundreds of years ago by psychiatrists who were most likely more obsessed with the sexual roots of the insanity, than curing the insanity itself. So then what are we left with to back up our right to draw this line in the sand between psychosis, neurosis and no "osis" at all? We're left with nothing except one man's word over another. The man that yells the loudest with the most circumstantial evidence is the man who defines what is a sane, correct reality, and the reality that we must live in, fake or face the consequences.

Let's face it, the reality we present to others is largely performance art with the script, criteria and stage directions set in place by societal expectations or our perception of them. Be free of addiction, without fear of intimacy, mentally balanced, perfectly sane, happy, regularly exercised, properly dieted, at a perfect weight, non-smoking, within a nuclear family, properly confronting life's challenges without callous ease and at the same time without significant difficulty. Only then can we be perfectly balanced people.

Faking it doesn't end with pretending we're flawless either. We fake our personalities – corporate team player, PTA parent, wife, kindly neighbor and more. Like actors of the Old Globe Theatre, we slap on the best mask for the situation. Unfortunately, most of the time, the mask we choose is one of neutrality and fortified contentment, rather than of personality and individuality. It's a mask that is the hardest to read and also the hardest to penetrate. It's the mask that in an instant can become whatever the audience that we are facing needs for it to be, so that their own mask doesn't seem out of place.

But do not be confused, this mask is not us. It is simply the world reflecting its needs and expectations onto us like some kind of co-dependent mirror. If they need it of themselves, they somehow expect that we will be able to give it unto them. We are truly faking the reality that society and others have thrust upon us and we have willingly or at the very least apathetically accepted. It's our reality – why do we have to fake it for the sake of other people's comfort level?

Quite simply, most of the time we do this to follow along with the script, not missing a beat. I've noticed that virtually every situation seems to have a "this is how it usually goes" dialogue that either I'm not interested in or am unaware of because nobody sent me the script in advance. I prefer the second choice. I would rather be surprised. Plus, I find that the pre-written scripts are often laced with dangerous subtext. With objectives ranging from passing time and waiting for one's chance to speak to looking for personal validation at the expense of the other person, I don't think that these scripts are doing us any favors.

Instead of using words to connect with and learn from each other, we are recycling the same words over and over, putting more and more distance between each other. Wednesday is hump day, TGIF, how are you, you know getting by, you know how it is, what can you do, I know tell me about it... This is so frustrating to me because the words that we use to express ourselves are the words we have either consciously or unconsciously pre-selected to represent who we are as the complex beings we supposedly are.

Think about those scripts and what they represent in your life. They are safe, correct and completely recycled from some stranger's personal uniqueness. These are words that may belong to us as a group, but that doesn't mean you have to adopt them as your own. Don't fake someone else's reality. Choose your own words and then own them. It's your reality, despite what others may have programmed you to believe through their words and actions. Make your own rules, choose the words that define and represent you and live it for real. What's the worst that could happen?

Why do we have to pretend to be perfect? How is perfection defined? Is it defined based on standards of consumption, addiction and behavioral norms? Who sets these standards? And what makes us feel as if we have to satisfy them? If we fail to follow the script, fake the reality and sell the correct performance, then God help us because the self-help deputies will have a warrant out for us. For our own good of course, we'll have to answer to them, explain how we could permit such imperfection, and make an immediate, heartfelt promise to change our evil ways and quickly rejoin the herd. We can do this or face the ultimate punishment – public shaming as an imperfect (human) being who has dared to reject the reality that everyone else has apparently accepted. This is the ultimate shame, the Scarlett Letter of modern times. To me the consequences of refusing to fake a reality are worth it. I celebrate my imperfections, political incorrectness, and insanity equally with my other life accomplishments and victories. This is my reality and faking it is not required.

Sexual Role Play...
Or Lesbianism II: Undercover experiences as a straight patron at a gay club

It's not Halloween, yet people are role playing all around me – the man, the woman, the gay, the straight, the dominant, submissive, the femme and the butch. They are playing them to the hilt, all aspects of the roles – the strategizing, conniving, ass grab, tender touch and so much more. How would an outsider know the difference? The mating ritual is the mating ritual. Animals are animals and people are people after all. Those who seek to separate us are those who fear their true colors and feelings for humanity will be revealed.

Humans need to connect with humans, no matter that the individual terms and conditions may dictate. God did create us as individuals after all. If he had desired a planet full of clones, herds of Barbie and Ken dolls would currently be streaming through subway tunnels, country roads and suburban neighborhoods worldwide.

To achieve these individualistic ends, these goals they have set as their ideal reality, people may alter their appearance, their physical gestures and their entire essence if they deem it to be necessary. Can any of us say that we are really different in that regard?

But what brought this particular group to this particular place? What brings a person of one born and raised gender to a place so far from their assumedly pre-destined anatomical role? And not just bringing them here, but so thoroughly convincing them of the rightness of this new existence? I can see it in their eyes – the mixture of fear of stepping outside the box while at the same time so fervently eager to see where this new yet familiar road leads. Or are those simply the familiar mix of emotions that come with all types of courtship and attraction? I suppose that would be dependent on the point of view of the observer - wouldn't it?

We all may have arrived at our own unique destination in life, but are we ever sure how it really happened? Does this particular group represent the breakdown or building up of the masses? If that is the question on the table, as it so often is allowed to be, then why aren't we asking it about any other group of people who have found different destinations in life from our own?

Meanwhile, at the club, a new group of outsiders takes mental tourist photos of what to them is a fantasy spectacle. They quickly drown out the honesty of the situation with their uncomfortable macho cat calls, liquor shots and preening. At first it is forbidden and enticing. Then, as the scene comes into focus and reality sets in, the realization that what at first seemed exotic and far fetched is quite simply a normal expression of desire. The newness fades and everyone returns to the safety of their own bubble.

Single by Choice...

My mother recently dropped an expression on me that apparently she picked up from her mother in the 1950's and subsequently forgot to take the time to figure out the meaning of: single by choice. The sister phrase of "old maid", my interpretation of the idea behind "single by choice" is that the poor gal had the *opportunity* to marry – gorgeous hunks on white horses lined up around the block every evening, begging the girl's father to trade her virtue for a flock of livestock – but, by principle she chose to remain single. This was apparently seen as a noble choice.

So let me get this straight, the opposite would be some hideous hag who, try as she might, couldn't find a single man on earth who would consider marrying her? This is awfully alarming, considering the motley mass of men populating the earth. Not a single one? Man, there must have been some ugly single women in the 1950's.

The other option, of course, spoken about in hushed suburban sewing circles, was the L word: "she must be a lesbian." This charming little fallacy has somehow survived the generations and still exists in retirement communities, where my mom's friends look at my naked fingers and seem to be on the fence between "single by choice" and "maybe she's one of those" (like it's some strange crossbred species). Well, absent the line of studs on white horses winding around the block to my mom's condo, they ask the question that I have developed the consummate answer for. The answer that I cheerfully provide invariably sends them fleeing back to their condos.

Are you married?

No ma'am.

Oh, well are you a (whispered) *'lesbian'*?

No, ma'am. If I was a lesbian I would be married to a lesbian.

Case closed.

P.S. If someone is a "virgin by choice" does that simply mean that whilst the young lady has been in the presence of an actual penis, she chose not to take action? Ah, the nobility of free choice.

Thin Gray Line...

How can we tell if we've crossed the line
From heaven to hell
The thing between
Black and white
Is not a place
Nor is it a being
It is no more real than the action we can take
when trapped there

Waspiest Wasp...

My name and basic stats are almost a dead giveaway -
Christine Elaine Whitmarsh from Auburn, MA.
White, Lutheran, and meat, vegetable and potato fed.
I am the waspiest wasp of all the wasps. So you'd
think...

Yes, my grandfather's ancestors date right back to the
Mayflower. That's right. We are a Scurvy proof
family to have survived that cruise ship from hell!
And people think Carnival sucks. There is also
grandma's side, bearers of Native American blood.

My best guess is that Grandpa's ancestors landed on Plymouth rock, disembarked, enjoyed a conjugal visit in a teepee and here I am today.

You should know that wasps are a paranoid breed, due to the inherent Puritan blood coursing through our veins. We all know that there's nobody more paranoid than a Puritan, right? You have a crazy neighbor? Turn off the lights and duck behind the couch. Puritans? They burn 'em. Crazy ex-girlfriend? Get a restraining order. Puritan? Fire up the BBQ!

Yes, my family has some of that paranoid Puritan blood, and since random pyromania is more frowned upon these days, we've had to channel our neuroses a little more productively. For me, that translates into OCD-like behaviors like washing my hands twenty-five times an hour and checking to make sure doors are locked just a few times before going to bed. Okay, so I'm Jack Nicholson in *As Good as it Gets*. In defense of my tics, let me introduce my mother, a WASP queen who makes Jewish mothers look like reckless, spendthrift Hiltons.

Some of my mom's paranoid pearls passed down to her daughters:

>Never sit on hotel bedspreads because people have sex on them!

>Always walk in circles around your car at night before getting in because there might be some maniac lying underneath waiting to slash your ankles. Or perhaps the freaky little kid in *Pet Semetery*.

>Always arrive early for Christmas Eve church service (around Thanksgiving) so you can get a good seat. Because everyone knows that church is like a rock concert: if you're not close enough for Jesus to drip blood on you, down in the first row mosh pit, then you're not a REAL fan!

This all comes from a woman whose safety procedure for a toaster fire was to throw the flaming toaster out the porch window into the backyard as all the neighbors watched, convinced that we truly were the ultimate cross between *Ozzy & Harriet* and *The*

Osbournes. My mother, the waspy creator of the flying flaming toaster!

When did we fall out of love with words?

Without words, life would be a never ending game of charades and Pictionary, minus the party pitchers of margaritas. The ability to speak and write language is one of those evolutionary cornerstones like opposable thumbs and fashion sense that separates us from our pets. Why then, are we subjected to the same recycled "if you're like me" marketing slogans, summer movies with the same plotlines and a noticeable lack of recent literary classics? Emails are puny portions of their predecessors, the handwritten letter, and business letters are post-it notes redirecting readers to graphic-laden flash websites. Is it me, or is the passion for creating new ways to express ourselves losing its pulse?

There are millions of words to choose from and unfortunately it's not as easy as a lottery drawing to pick the perfect phrases for the particular people you hope to impress. Like it or not, words are how we learn, love, impact, and reach out to each other. You don't have to be Shakespeare to have a healthy appreciation of the beauty and possibilities of language. But channeling his spirit might be a good start. That guy understood the power of language versus literary shortcuts. After all, what if Juliet had told Romeo that she would "BRB"? LOL.

Reconnecting with your inner words...

Write one sentence about who you were, for a time capsule that will be opened 100 years from now.

Start a journal – a free speech zone for your words. Share it with the world via blogging, emails, t-shirts, buttons, voicemails, a book, bumper stickers – share it. It is okay to do this.

V.

LAST WORDS

Last words…

>Learning from the past does not mean living in it.

>You are the sole proprietor of your time. Don't let anyone sublet it without your express permission.

>Always put worth behind your words.

>Innate curiosity makes hatred very difficult.

>My favorite word is catecholamine. It's the name of the chemical that your body releases when you laugh, that subsequently builds up your immune system and makes you healthy. I hope that I've helped to release just a little bit of this wonder drug in you, possibly warding off the next sickness that someone sneezes on you.

>If you don't think that you have an interesting life perhaps it's because you've chosen not to be interested in life.

And in Closing…

I sincerely hope that the honesty and candor of my personal looking glass into the world will motivate you to dig down and unearth your own honest potpourri of thoughts, observations, curiosities, opinions, theories, comedies and complaints - your words.

Only when we begin to be honest with ourselves about our words will we have the power to use them to shape and shift the direction of our world. Our individual, community, national and global words have infinitely more power than simple dotted "i's", crossed "t's" and grammatically perfect sentences.

Human beings are the sole life forms with the capability to act as an intellectual, creative and operational axis of this planet. If we change directions from human progress to a plateau of intellectual stagnation, then we really will regress back to cave days. We will desperately strive to communicate with each other and future generations cratching images of times gone by on stone walls; Images that reflect a mere skeleton of the hopes, dreams, ideals and future of an entire civilization. Images that, while effective for what they are, will never have the power to replace the only medium ever created that allows a civilization to achieve its greatest potential. The only force that allows us to truly be the authors of our own destiny and the destinies of those who come after us - is WORDS.

Our words are intellectual and philosophical byproducts of our states as evolved beings. Without language, we have little to no hope of progressing any further than we have already. An artist's legacy can be left in images of beauty. A musician's is in the most melodic of melodies. However the legacy of words is not owned exclusively by authors. Words are an evolving time capsule, carrying entire chapters of history from one generation to the next.

Words don't deserve the kind of death that is imminent for them if we don't start appreciating their significance. Language has given us so much. Let's resuscitate it before it's too late and we are, once again, scratching stick pictures on stone walls, praying desperately for a better way to connect with one another.

You are a citizen of this world. You may not always feel like you're completely connected to all the noise, static, chaos, wild untamed energy, and insanity flying around you, but you absolutely are. The words in your head, heart and soul are your opinions. They are real, they are honest, and they are worthy of sharing.

If we can't share our words with each other... well, then, who can we share them with? What are you waiting for? Citizens of the world – speak up!